Rev-o-LOOM-tion

A Modern Kids Guide to Rocking Rubber Bands

Liz Hum

This book is available in quantity at special discounts for your group or organization. For further information, contact:

Triumph Books LLC
814 North Franklin Street
Chicago, Illinois 60610
Phone: (312) 337-0747
www.triumphbooks.com

Printed in U.S.A.

ISBN: 978-1-60078-999-1

Content developed and packaged by Rockett Media, Inc.
Writer: Liz Hum
Editor: Bob Baker
Design: Liz Hum
Cover Design by Liz Hum

Rev-o-LOOM-tion

What's the deal

With endless color combinations and styles you can customize yourself, it's no wonder that rubber band jewelry is the hottest trend right now. And the best part is you are in control, because you are the designer! Whether it's a heavy metal cuff, a trendy choker, or a flower child ring, you can make anything to suit your mood.

And it all started with weaving. Weaving is the process of interlacing threads to make cloth and it has been around since the dawn of civilization. From braiding hair to making clothing, rugs, and baskets, it is an incredibly useful skill.

A LOOM is a tool that facilitates weaving. At first, people used simple hand looms to hold vertical threads (called warp) in place while they weaved a separate thread (called a weft) horizontally, through them. As weaving became more popular, Edmund Cartwright invented the power loom to keep up with the growing demand for textiles and woven items.

During the Industrial Revolution (when we first began using factories and machines to produce goods), women used to work for long hours in front of huge, deafeningly-loud looms. They would have to wear handkerchiefs over their noses because all the dust caused lung problems. The machines were very dangerous and injured many weavers. Girls around the age of 14 would get special slips to get out of school early and apprentice with the older women. Can you imagine having to work in a factory from afternoon until dinnertime?

with the LOOM?

These days, looming is done in cleaner, safer factories by skilled laborers who work about 40-48 hours a week. The use of cheaper labor, synthetic materials, and robotic machinery is causing a decline in looming jobs. This means fewer and fewer people will ever learn how to weave, so it is important to keep this knowledge alive. Arts and crafts is a fun way to do that!

Weaving rugs and clothing and baskets by hand is still practiced by Native Americans and indigenous people in South and Central America, Africa, and throughout Asia. Some artists travel to these places to learn the skill from master artisans.

When you use a hand loom, you learn how two threads lace together to make something stronger. It improves your manual dexterity (your hand speed) and your concentration, and it has a calming effect. Once you get the hang of it, you can rely on yourself to make something your way, instead of buying something that isn't "quite" what you wanted.

So, when you start rocking these rubber band bracelets, remember, you're not just making super-cool accessories and one-of-a-kind jewelry. You are learning a very old and vital skill that you can build upon to make almost anything you set your mind to!

Did You Know?

The inventor of the Rainbow Loom ® is a man named Choon Ng, who came up with the idea for the tool because his fingers were too big to make the simple rubber band bracelets his daughters were weaving by hand.

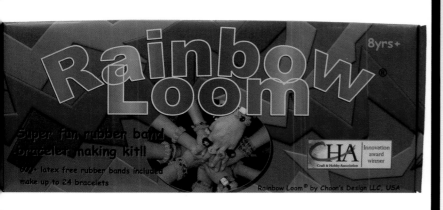

Before You Begin...

So, you just opened your new rubber band loom and want to rock 'n' roll. Not so fast! Before you start setting and looping, you must keep these things in mind:

First, you need to organize your rubber bands by color. You can get a divided utility box from your local craft store for this exact purpose. It will take you FOREVER to pick out colors for a pattern if they aren't neatly separated. (Keep one divider of rainbow-colored bands, too, just in case you feel spontaneous.)

It is very important to have a clean workspace. A good idea would be a clean desk or table where other people can't bump into you or spill anything on your project. You don't want to wear or give a bracelet with crumbs and strands of hair stuck in it. That's just gross. (Tip: tie your hair back, too.)

Each design in this book is labeled according to its level of difficulty. The three levels are: Easy-Peasy, for those just learning how to loom, Rockin' Rainbows, for those who are ready for more complicated patterns, and LOOM-a-tic, for the pros. It is best to accomplish each design in order, as one builds upon the next.

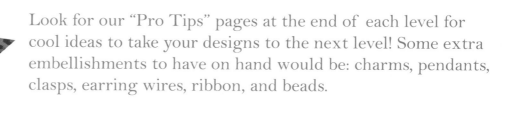

4. Look for our "Pro Tips" pages at the end of each level for cool ideas to take your designs to the next level! Some extra embellishments to have on hand would be: charms, pendants, clasps, earring wires, ribbon, and beads.

5. Each design follows the same principles. First you SET the rubber bands (the red arrow will point away) in a specific, overlapping pattern. Then, you place a CAP BAND (a rubber band doubled over on itself) on a certain peg or pegs to keep your bands from falling apart. Finally, you turn the loom around completely (the red arrow will point towards you) and begin to LOOP the bands back over one another.

6. Look at the pegs on your loom and look at your hook. When you are SETTING, the pegs will be closed. When you are LOOPING, there is an open channel in each peg. If you point your hook into that open space, it will be easier to hook the right rubber band.

7. It can be very frustrating when you realize you forgot one loop and your whole design falls apart when you try to take it off of the loom. It happens to all of us at one point or another. Sometimes a rubber band snaps after you spent hours weaving. It can make you want to scream! But remember, take a deep breath, a small break, and start over. You will be surprised at how much better you are each time you try!

Level: Easy-Peasy

The "Single" is the simplest loop design. Conquer this first to get the hang of the basics.

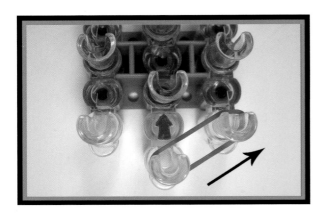

1. Lay the loom in front of you, with the red arrow pointing away from you. Stretch a rubber band from the very first peg in the middle to the first side peg, as shown.

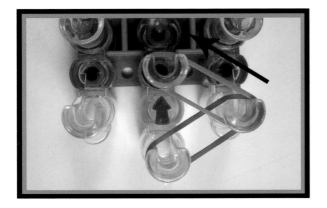

2. Stretch another rubber band from the first side peg to the second middle peg.

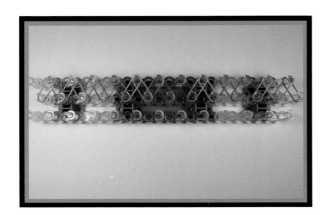

3. Continue laying the rubber bands in an overlapping, zig-zag fashion, until you reach the last peg on the loom.

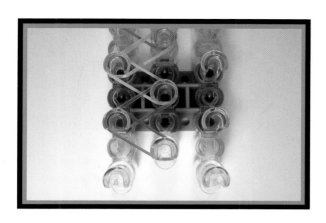

4. Turn the loom around so the red arrow is pointing towards you.

5. Guide your hook into the peg, so that the hook end points into the peg, and pick the second rubber band from underneath the first. Pull to release it from the peg.

6. Loop the rubber band onto the next peg, moving backwards through your zig-zag. Try not to twist up the rubber band when you do this, or your bracelet will get twist-y as well. Fold it over as flat as you can.

7. Again, guide your hook into the next peg and grab the next rubber band.

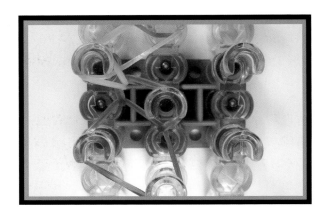

8. Loop it forward onto the next peg. You are essentially linking each band onto the next to form a chain.

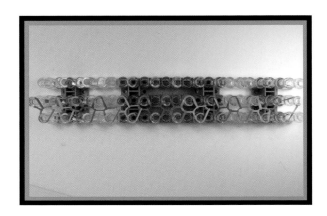

9. Repeat steps 4 and 5 along the loom, all the way to the opposite end (the side you started on).

10. Pull the two folds of the band from your last loop out, but not off the loom, with your hook and attach a c-clip. Make sure the clip secures both bands.

11. Starting with the clip end, gently pull the rubber bands from the loom with a side-to-side upward tugging motion. Secure the other side to the c-clip and BAM! You have accomplished "The Single."

Triple-Single

Level: Easy-Peasy

The "Triple-Single" takes the setting and looping process a step forward by adding rows, making it the simplest of the thick bracelets.

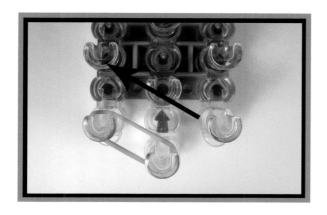

1. Begin with the loom's red arrow pointing away from you. Set your first rubber band from the first center peg out to the first peg on the left side.

2. Continue to set bands all the way up the left column of pegs.

TIP: Set the bands to the middle of each peg, so there is room for more bands on top. We will be adding another layer.

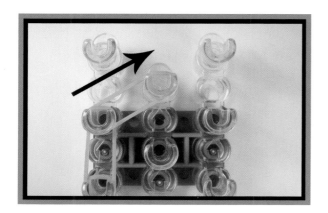

3. At the end, skip the last peg on the left and instead set your band around the last middle peg.

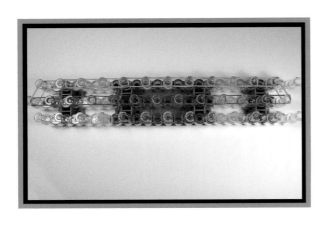

4. Now, set a row of rubber bands up the middle in the same overlapping fashion, all the way to the last middle peg.

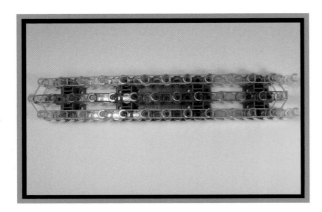

5. Repeat steps 1-3 on the right side of the loom.

6. Place a cap band on the last middle peg. Do this by twisting and folding one rubber band, so that it doubles, and place it on top of the last middle peg, where the three rubber bands meet.

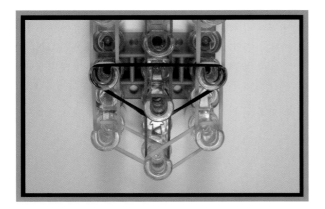

7. Next, we add a row of triangles across the loom. Skip the first three pegs, and wrap a rubber band across the second set of three pegs, as shown.

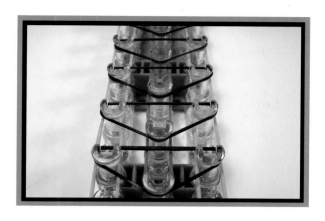

8. Continue placing triangles up the loom.

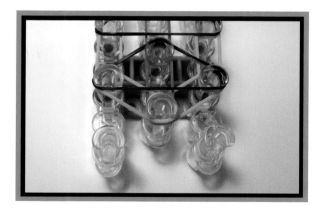

9. The final triangle should be placed before the cap band.

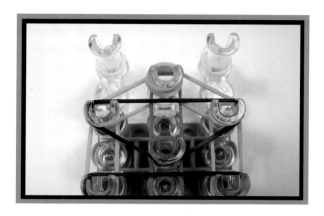

10. Turn the loom around, so the red arrow is pointing towards you.

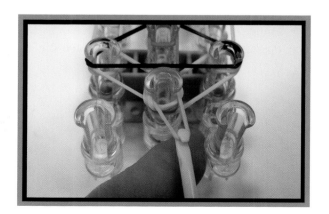

11. Guide your hook through the hole in the center of the first middle peg. Position the hook to face into the peg and the flat end to face toward you. Use the flat side to push the cap bands back as you hook the first band underneath them.

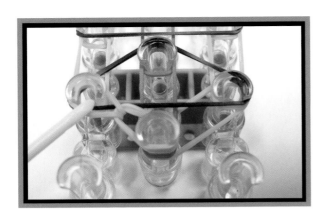

12. Release the band, without removing the cap band, and loop it to the first peg on the left side.

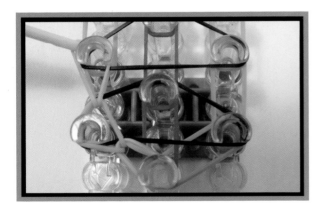

13. Again, guide your hook into the next peg the same way. Push the triangle band and the looped bands back so you can hook the rubber band underneath it.

14. Loop it onto the next peg.

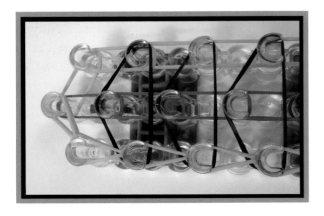

15. Repeat looping the bands all the way up the left side and loop the last rubber band to the last middle peg.

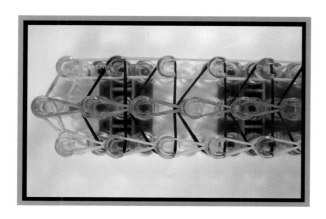

16. Next, repeat the looping process up the center row. Be careful not to accidentally hook the cap band on your first loop.

17. Repeat steps 11-15 on the right side of your loom. Again, push the triangle bands back with the flat end of your hook so that you only catch the bottom bands.

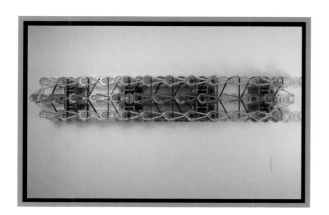

18. When the looping is completed, your loom should look like this. If it doesn't, or if you notice one band making an odd shape, go back and see if you can fix it. If not, the best thing to do is take a breath and start over.

19. Turn your loom around, so that the red arrow is pointing away from you. Slide your hook down the center peg, making sure it is down the center of every looped band and tilt it outward.

20. Hook a rubber band onto your hook and pull it through the center of the bands.

21. Slide both sides of the band to the thick part of your hook.

22. Use the hook to pull the bracelet off of the loom. Pull backwards and upwards, using a side-to-side motion.

23. When complete, your bracelet will not be long enough for a typical wrist, so it must be finished with extensions. Leave the bracelet on your hook for the moment, and loop 4-6 bands along the right side of your loom.

24. Take your cap band, from the opposite side of the bracelet that is still on the hook, and loop it around the last two pegs.

25. With your fingers under the bands on your hook (so they don't slip off), loop the extension bands over, starting with the band under your cap band, just like you did with the "Single" bracelet.

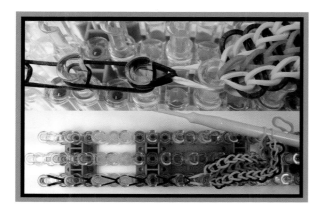

26. Loop them until the end.

27. Hook the last loop and wrap it around the middle peg, as shown. Attach a c-clip.

28. Pull it off of the loom, by the c-clip. Stretch the hook bands out with your finger and attach the other end of the c-clip to finish.

29. Voila! You have accomplished the "Triple Single" bracelet.

Diamond

The "Diamond" design is a thinner band with double the depth and complexity of the "Single."

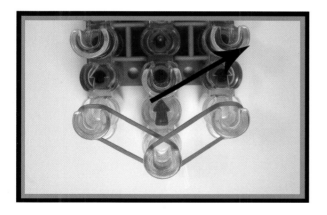

1. Start with the red arrow pointing away from you. Set your first band from the first middle peg to the first peg on the left.

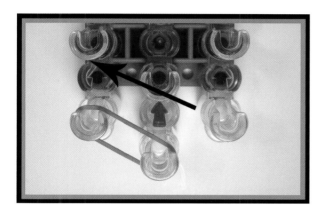

2. Set your second rubber band from the first middle peg to the first peg on the right.

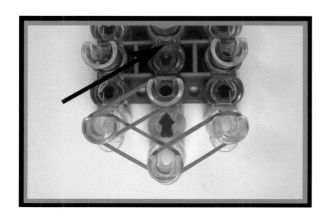

3. Set your third rubber band from the first peg on the left to the second peg in the middle.

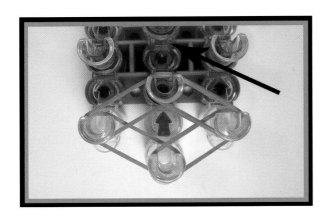

4. Set your fourth rubber band from the first peg on the right to the second peg in the middle, completing a diamond-shaped pattern.

TIP: Make sure you push all the bands down for easy layering. Don't let the bands twist.

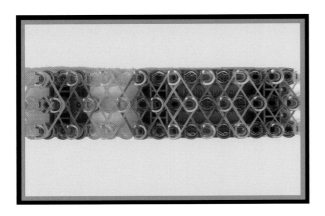

5. Repeat the pattern (middle to left, middle to right, left to middle, right to middle) all the way up the loom.

6. End at the last middle peg. Check your bands and make sure there is some extra room at the top of the peg for looping. Push them down again, if necessary.

7. Place a cap band on the last peg, by twisting a rubber band and doubling it over, then sliding it on top of the other bands.

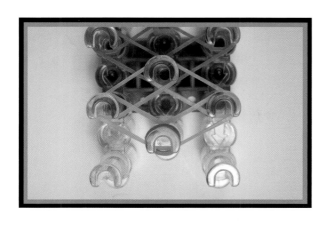

8. Turn your loom around so that the red arrow is pointing towards you.

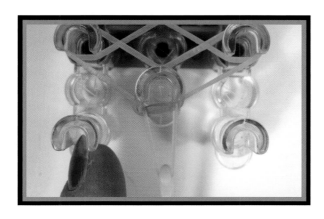

9. Guide your hook into the peg, with the hook side pointing in, and push the cap band out to hook the first rubber band underneath it.

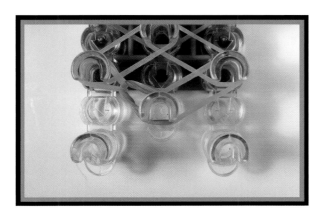

10. Loop it to the first peg on the left.

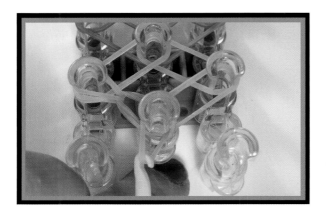

11. Guide your hook into the peg, with the hook side pointing in, and push the cap band out to hook the next rubber band underneath it.

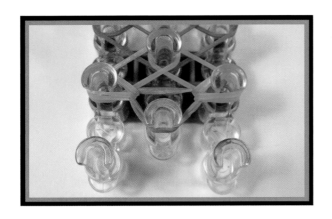

12. Loop it to the first peg on the right.

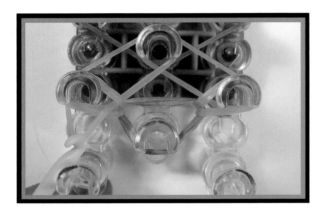

13. Guide your hook into the left peg, with the hook side pointing in, and push the already looped band out of the way to hook the next rubber band underneath it.

14. Loop it up to the next center peg.

15. Guide your hook into the right peg, with the hook side pointing in, and push the already looped band out of the way to hook the next rubber band underneath it.

16. Loop it to the same center peg.

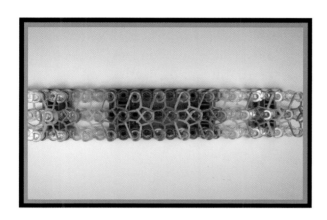

17. Following the same pattern you set the rubber bands with (middle-left, middle-right, left-middle, right-middle), continue looping all the rubber bands to the end of your loom. Be careful, especially on the middle pegs, not to grab any of the previously looped bands by accident.

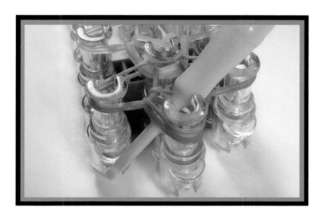

18. Turn your loom around, so that the red arrow is pointing away from you. Slide your hook down the first center peg, making sure it is down the center of every looped band and tilt it outward.

19. Hook a rubber band onto your hook and pull it through the center of the bands.

20. Slide both sides of the band to the thick part of your hook.

21. Use the hook to pull the bracelet off of the loom, using an upwards and backwards, side-to-side motion.

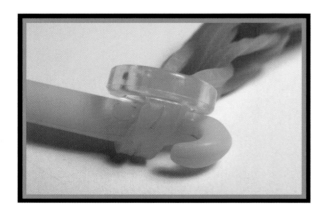

22. Attach a c-clip to the bands looped on your hook.

23. Connect the last band to the c-clip and you have a "Diamond" bracelet!

Ladder

Level: Easy-Peasy

The "Ladder" is one of the simplest thick bracelets with three full layers of rubber bands.

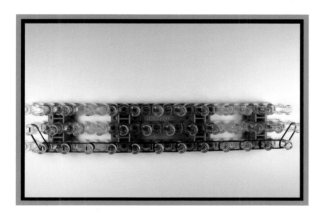

1. Begin with the loom's red arrow towards you. Loop your first rubber band from the first center peg out to the first peg on the left side.

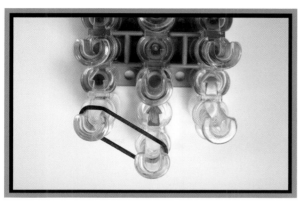

2. Continue to loop bands all the way up the left column of pegs.

Tip: loop the bands to the middle of each peg, not too high, so the upper-layer of bands will fit easily. (We will be adding another layer.)

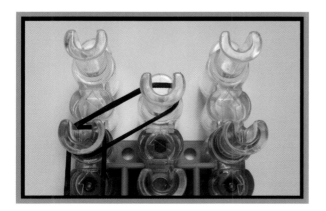

3. At the end, skip the last peg on the left and instead loop your band around the last middle peg.

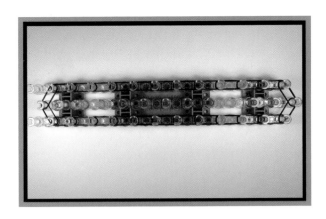

Repeat steps 1-3 on the right side of the loom.

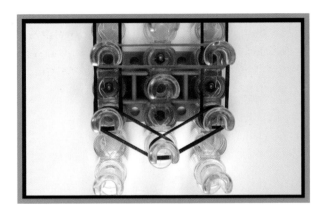

Set a band from the second left peg to the second right peg.

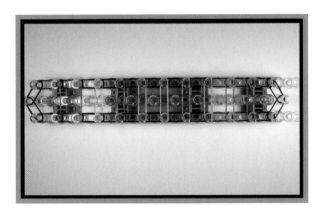

Repeat up the loom. Just like the beginning of the pattern, do not place a band over the last two pegs. Then push all of wyour bands down for the next layers.

Starting with the first peg in the center, stretch a row of bands all the way up the middle column of the loom.

8. Turn your loom around, so the red arrow is pointing towards you, and place a cap band on the middle peg. Do this by twisting and folding one rubber band, so that it doubles, and place it on top of the last middle peg, where the three rubber bands meet.

9. Guide your hook through the hole in the peg. Position the hook to face into the peg and the flat end to face toward you. Use the flat side to push the cap bands back as you hook the band underneath them.

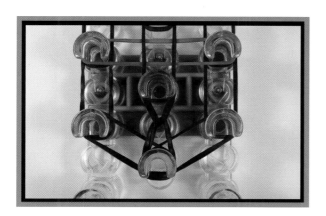

10. Release the band, without removing the cap band, and loop it to the next middle peg.

11. Continue looping all the way up the center of the loom.

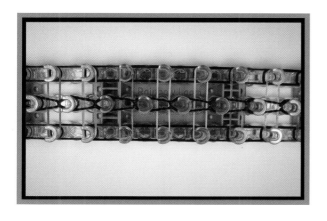

12. Go back to the beginning and lay another row of horizontal bands on top of the first, as shown. These are your "ladder" rungs.

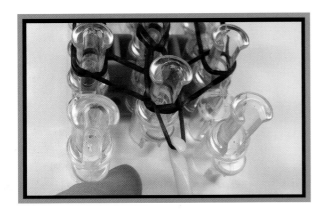

13. Guide your hook through the hole in the first center peg. Position the hook to face into the peg and the flat end to face toward you. Use the flat side to push the cap bands back as you hook the first band underneath them.

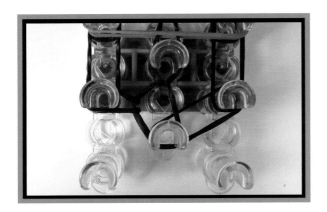

14. Release the band, without removing the cap band, and loop it to the first peg on the left side.

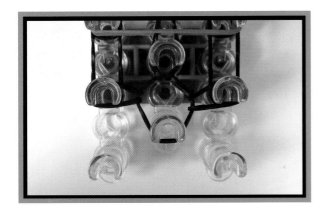

15. Repeat on the right side.

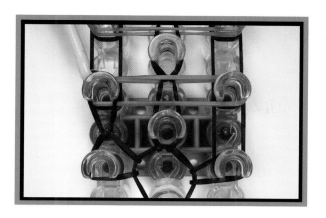

16. On the left side, loop the lowest band to the next peg.

17. Continue looping up the left side of the loom, being careful to only hook the bottom band and loop it to the following peg. You will have to push both layers of ladder rungs out of the way to do this.

TIP: It becomes very important to make sure your bands have been pushed down to accommodate layers on top. It is also important to keep every layer spaced in the order it was placed.

18. Repeat steps 15-16 on the right side of your loom.

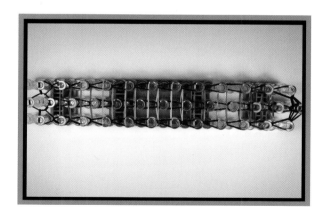

19. Turn your loom around, so that the red arrow is pointing away from you. Slide your hook down the center peg, making sure it is down the center of every looped band and tilt it outward.

20. Hook a rubber band onto your hook and pull it through the center of the bands.

21. Slide both sides of the band to the thick part of your hook.

22. Use the hook to pull the bracelet off of the loom, using an upwards and backwards, side-to-side motion.

23. This bracelet will need to be extended. Set 4-6 bands along the right side of your loom. Place your cap band on the last set of overlapping pegs.

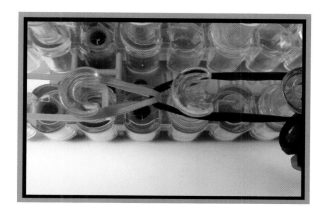

24. With your fingers under the bands on your hook (so they don't slip off), loop the singles over, starting with the band under your cap band.

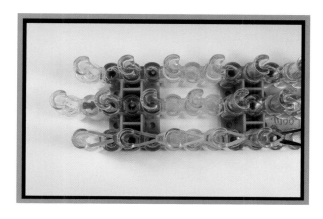

25. Loop them until the end.

26. Hook the last loop and wrap it around the middle peg, as shown, and attach a c-clip.

27. Pull it off of the loom, by the c-clip. Stretch the hook bands out with your finger and attach the other end of the c-clip to finish.

Easy-Peasy Level
PRO TIPS

Use two rubber bands instead of one, for a thicker look!

Connect two looms together (See page 66, "Hacking your Loom") to turn your extension-requiring designs into full, wrap-around bracelets.

Make a beaded ladder bracelet by adding only one row of "rungs" and fishing two pony beads onto each one.

In fact, try adding beads to the other designs and bling them out!

Pony beads are easy to start with because of their size. You can buy them at any craft store.

Serpentine

Level: Rockin' Rainbows

The "Serpentine" is a little more challenging and introduces an 8-step pattern. The result is a snakelike twist around a straight, thin bracelet.

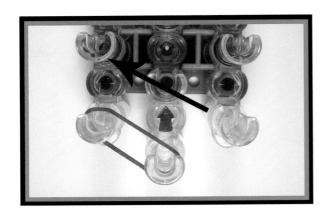

1. Start with the loom's arrow pointing away from you. Set your first band from the first middle peg to the first left peg.

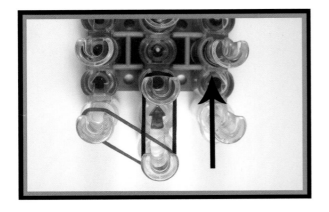

2. Set your second rubber band from the first middle peg to the second middle peg.

TIP: Use the same color for every band you place up the center column. This will be the "pole" that the "snake" is twisting around.

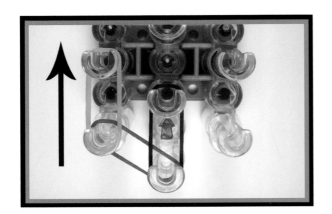

3. Place your third band from the first left peg to the second left peg.

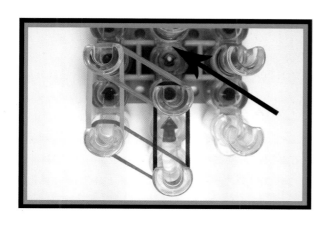

4. Set your fourth band from the second center peg out to the second left peg.

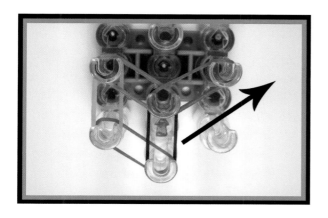

5. Set your fifth band from the second center peg out to the second peg on the right.

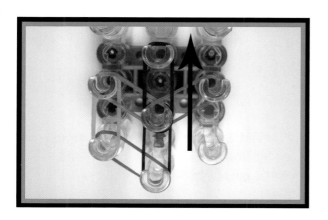

6. Set your sixth band from the second middle peg to the third middle peg. Again, use the same color you used for your second band to achieve the full finished effect.

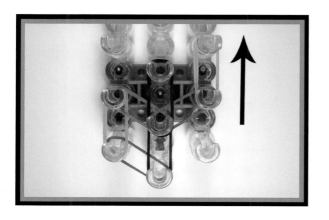

7. Set your seventh band from the second right peg to the third right peg.

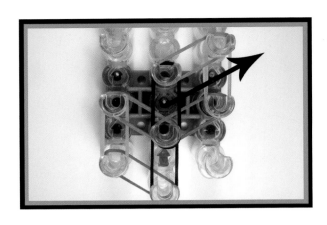

8. Set your eighth band from the third middle peg out to the third right peg.

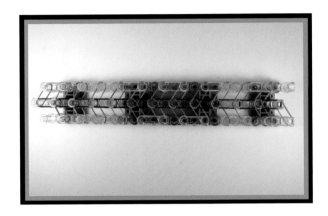

9. Repeat this 8-step pattern all the way up your loom, in the exact order.

10. Turn your loom around, so the red arrow points towards you, and place a cap band on the center peg.

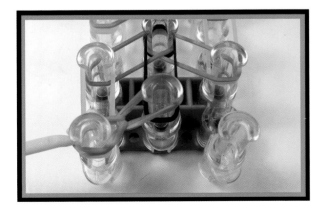

11. Guide your hook into the center peg and hook the first band underneath the cap band. Loop it down to the first peg on the left.

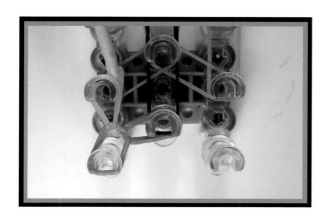

12. Guide your hook into the first left peg and loop that band to the second left peg.

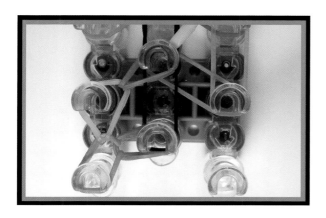

13. Guide your hook into the second left peg and loop the band up to the second peg in the center.

14. Go back to the first middle peg and loop that band straight up to the second middle peg.

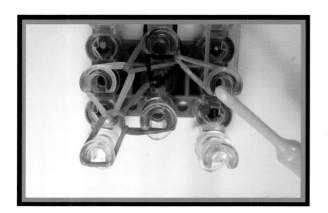

15. Guide your hook into the second center peg and hook the band stretching to the right. Loop it down to the second peg on the right.

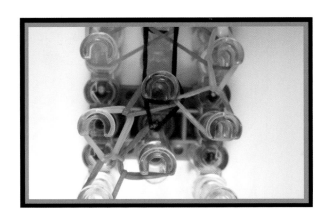

16. Guide your hook into the second right peg and loop that band to the third right peg.

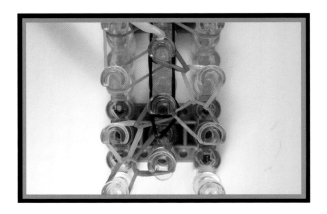

17. Guide your hook into the third right peg and loop the band up into the third peg in the center.

18. Go back to the second middle peg and loop that band straight up to the third middle peg.

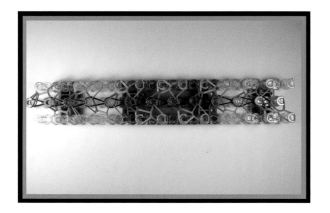

19. Repeat looping the snake-like pattern in the same order all the way up the loom.

20. Hook a new rubber band through your loose bands on the last center peg to hold them together.

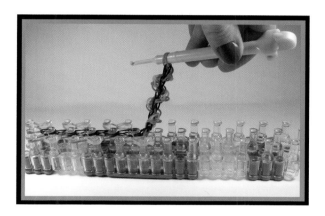

21. Lift your bracelet off the loom.

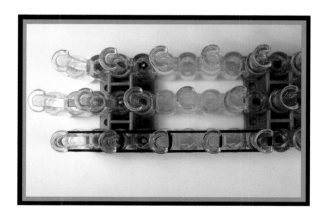

22. If you used one loom, you will need to extend the bracelet by looping 4-6 bands along the right side of your loom.

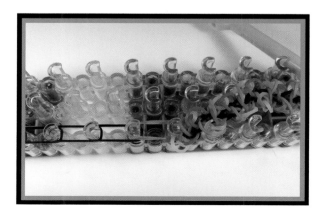

23. Stretch your cap band across the last two pegs.

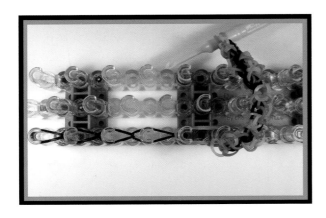

24. Loop the extensions all the way down.

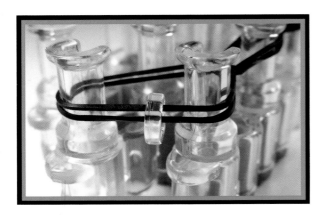

25. Add your c-clip to the last loop.

26. Connect the sides and you have yourself a snaking "Serpentine" bracelet!

Level: Rockin' Rainbows

The "Starburst" pattern is a more complicated bracelet with multiple layers which end up fanning out in all directions.

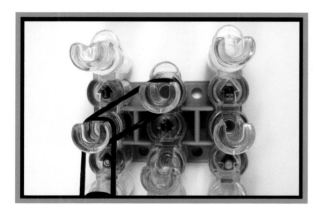

1. Start with the loom's arrow pointing away from you. Place your first band from the first center peg to the first left peg and continue all the way up the left side.

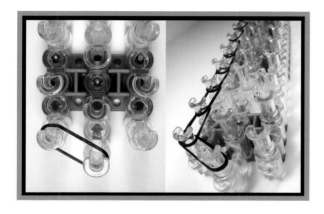

2. The last band should stretch from the 12th left peg to the last middle peg.

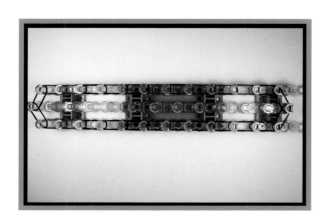

3. Repeat steps 1 & 2 on the right side of your loom.

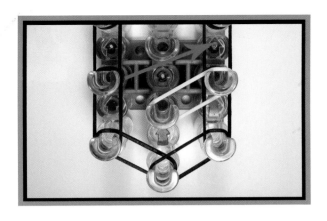

4. To begin placing the starburst, set a band from the second center peg to the second right peg.

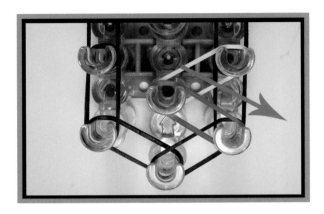

5. Set your second band from the second center peg to the first right peg.

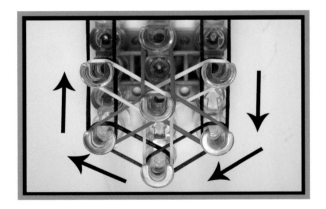

6. Set the remaining four bands clockwise from the center. You will need to push the bands down on the center peg for easy layering.

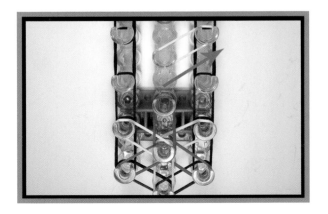

7. To place your next starburst, begin at the fourth center peg and extend your band to the fourth right peg.

8. Set your second band from the fourth middle peg to the third right peg.

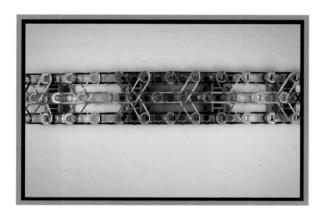

9. Set the remaining four bands the same way, clockwise from the center.

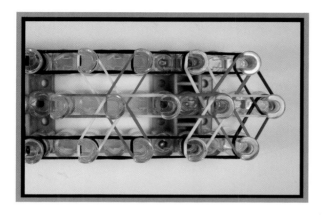

10. Continue this pattern, in the exact order, all the way up your loom.

11. Place a cap band on the last center peg.

12. Next, place a cap band on the center of each starburst, all the way across the loom.

13. Turn the loom around, so the red arrow is pointing towards you, and guide your hook under the cap band to pick the first starburst petal.

14. Loop it to the center.

15. Move your hook up to the center of the first starburst. Guide your hook under the cap band, and pull out the top band, underneath it.

16. Loop it down to the second right peg.

17. Guide your hook back under the cap band, into the center of the first starburst pattern, and pull out the next top band, underneath the cap band.

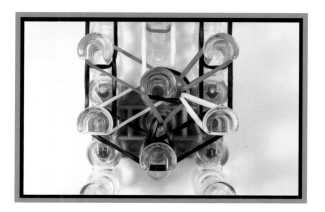

18. Loop it to the third right peg.

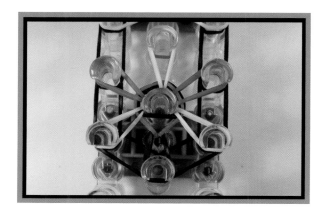

19. Finish looping all the starburst petals in a counter-clockwise direction. Be careful to only hook the correct band. Use your fingers and the hook to press back any other layers. Push them down on the loom, if necessary.

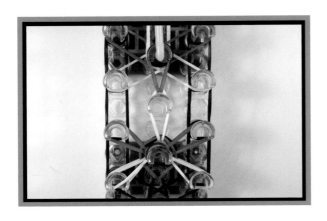

20. Loop the first petal of your second starburst by pulling the band from the fourth middle peg and looping it up to the fifth middle peg, the center of your next starburst.

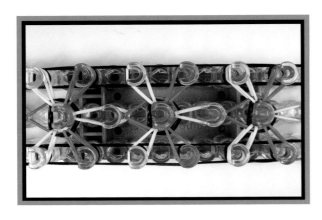

21. Again, finish looping all the rest of the starburst petals from the center outward, in the same counter-clockwise direction. Make sure you are guiding your hook underneath each cap band when looping. The starbursts should look like this picture.

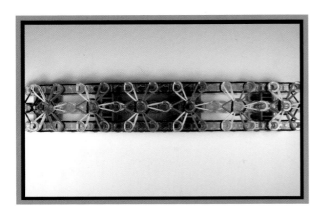

22. Repeat the exact same pattern in the exact same order, all the way up your loom.

23. Next, loop the perimeter bands, by guiding your hook down the center peg, under the cap band, and hooking the first band. Loop it to the next peg on the left.

24. Continue looping the bottom bands all the way up the left side of the loom.

25. Loop the last band to the final middle peg.

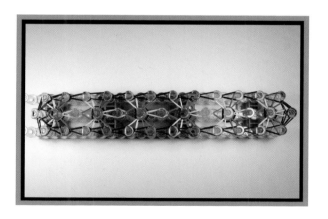

26. Repeat on the right side.

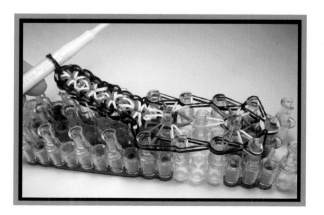

27. Hook a rubber band through the loose loops on the last peg, slide it up your hook, and pull the bracelet from the loom.

28. If you used one loom, extend the bracelet by looping 4-6 extra bands up the side of your loom and wrapping your cap band over the last two pegs.

29. Loop them back over one another and add a c-clip to the last loop.

30. Attach the end from your hook to the other side of the c-clip.

31. Show off your sweet "Starburst"!

Flowers

Level: Rockin' Rainbows

The "Flowers" pattern creates a thick band of rosettes. Where the Starburst has a straight border, the Flower's edges are curved around each segment.

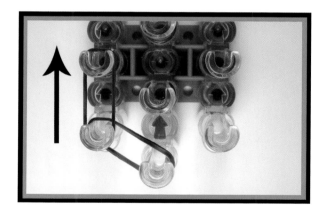

1. Start with the loom's red arrow pointing away from you. Begin a hexagon shape by setting your first rubber band from the first middle peg out to the first left peg.

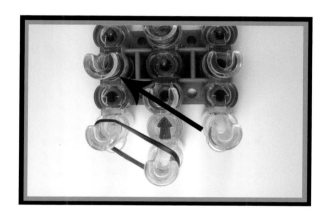

2. Set the next band from the first left peg to the second left peg.

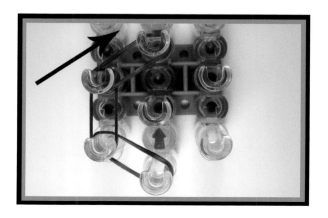

3. Set your third band from the second left peg to the third middle peg.

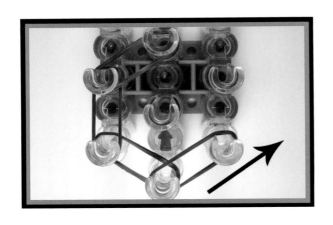

4. Set your fourth rubber band from the first middle peg to the first right peg.

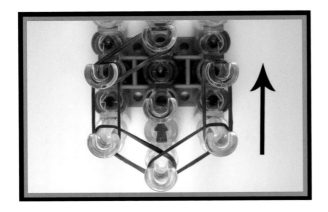

5. Set your fifth band from the first right peg to the second right peg.

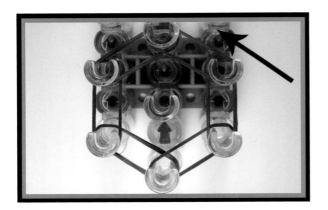

6. Set your sixth rubber band from the second right peg to the third middle peg.

7. Repeat this hexagon pattern all the way up your loom in the exact order, three up the left side, then three up the right side.

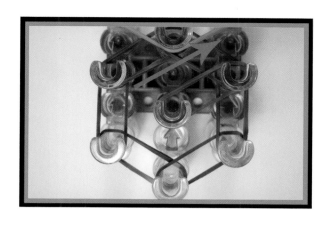

8. Begin the flower by setting a band from the center peg of the first hexagon out to second left peg.

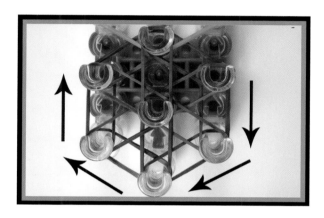

9. Set the rest of your bands clockwise from the center

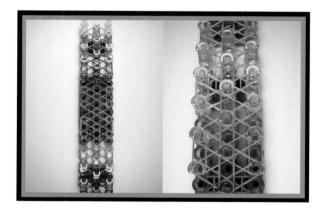

10. Repeat that pattern exactly, laying a flower in each hexagon, all the way up the loom.

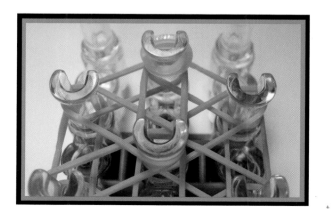

11. Place a cap band on the last center peg.

12. Place a cap band in the center of each flower, all the way across the loom.

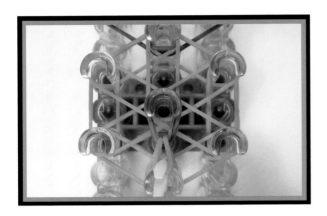

13. Turn your loom around, so the arrow is pointing toward you, and guide your hook through the center of the flower, under the cap band. Hook the first band underneath it.

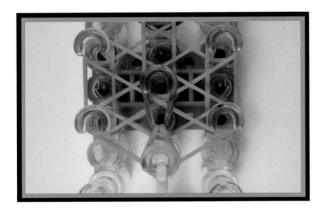

14. Loop it straight down to the middle peg below.

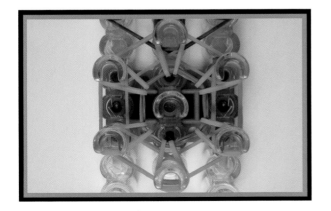

15. Loop the rest of the bands from the middle in a counter-clockwise direction.

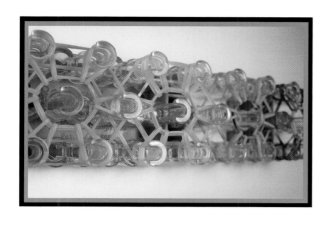

16. Repeat the same pattern, in the same order, counter-clockwise from the middle of each flower.

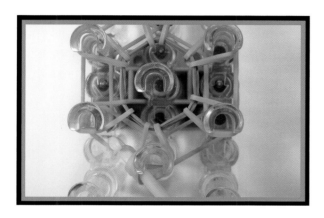

17. Seal the hexagon back up by guiding your hook down into the first middle peg and catching the second-to-bottom band.

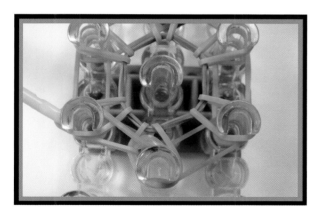

18. Loop it to the left peg.

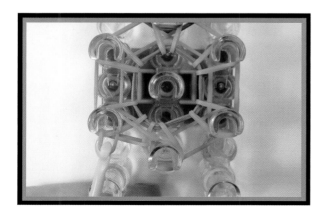

19. Guide your hook into the second left peg and pull the bottom band.

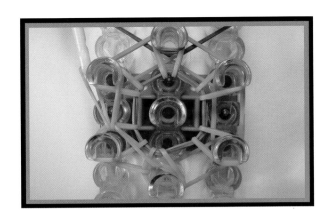

20. Loop it up one peg.

21. Guide your hook into the third left peg and pull the bottom band.

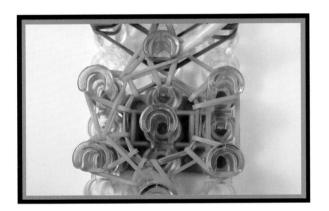

22. Loop it to the third middle peg.

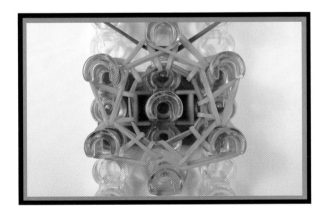

23. Follow the same steps up the right side of your hexagon.

24. Repeat sealing each hexagon around each flower, all the way up your loom.

25. Loop a rubber band through the last peg to seal the end, push it up your hook, and pull the bracelet from the loom.

26. If you used one loom, extend the bracelet by setting 4-6 extra bands up the side of your loom and wrapping your cap band over the last two pegs.

27. Loop them back over one another and add a c-clip to the last loop.

28. Attach the end from your hook to the other side of the c-clip and feel the flower power!

Diamond Rings

Level: Rockin' Rainbows

The "Diamond Rings" choker incorporates two bracelet-sized pieces to make one continuous necklace with a lace-like effect.

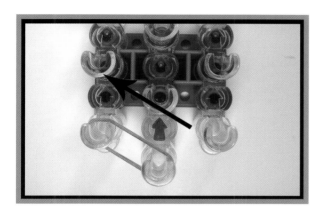

1. Begin with the loom's red arrow pointing away from you. Place your first rubber band from the first middle peg to the first left peg.

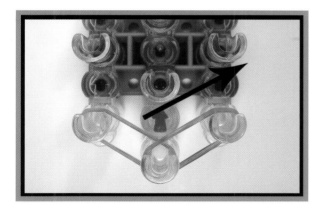

2. Place your second rubber band from the first middle peg to the first right peg.

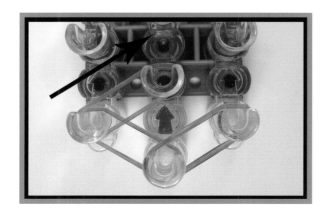

3. Place your third rubber band from the first left peg to the second middle peg.

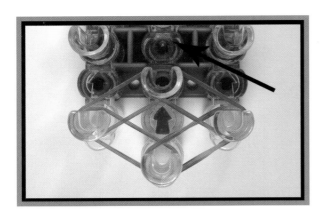

4. Set your fourth rubber band from the first right peg to the second middle peg to form a diamond shape.

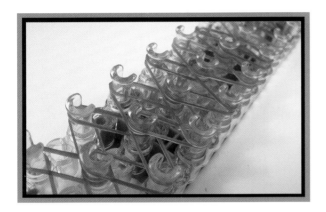

5. Repeat the diamond-shaped pattern in this exact order, all the way up your loom.

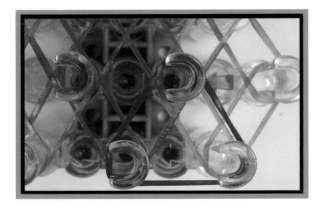

6. Go back to the beginning. Stretch a band across the first left peg, second left peg, and the second middle peg to form a triangle.

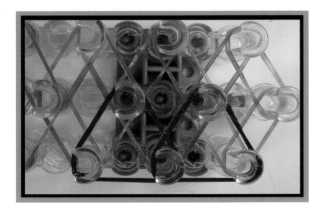

7. Place another triangle from the second left peg to the third left peg and the third middle peg, so the triangles overlap at the corner.

8. Continue setting triangles all the way up the left side of your loom.

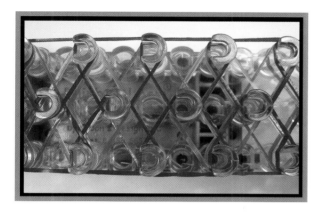

9. Repeat steps 6-8 on the right side of your loom.

10. Place a cap band on your last middle peg and push all the bands down along your loom.

11. Turn your loom around and guide your hook into the center peg. Pull the top band out from under the cap band.

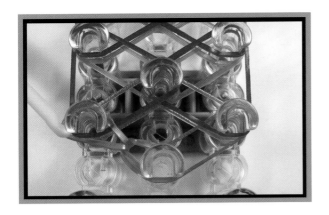

12. Loop it to the left peg.

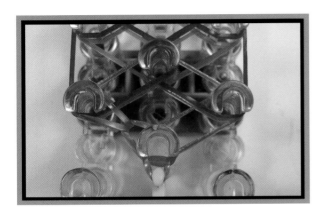

13. Go back to the center peg and guide your hook in to catch the bottom band under the cap band.

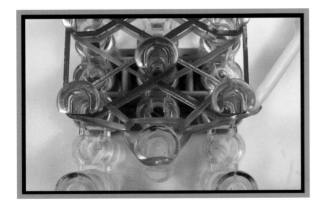

14. Loop it over to the right peg.

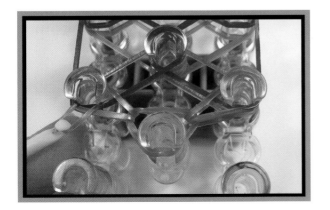

15. Guide your hook into the next left peg and pull out the bottom band.

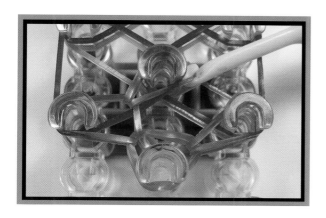

16. Loop it to the next middle peg.

17. Guide your hook into the next right peg and pull out the bottom band.

18. Loop it to the same middle peg that you looped the left band.

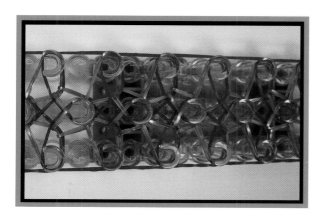

19. Continue looping in this order, middle to left, middle to right, left to middle, right to middle, all the way to the other side. Loop through the triangles, but do not remove them from their pegs.

20. Guide your hook through the last peg to grab all the bands. Loop a rubber band through them and push it to the thick part of your hook. Pull the whole piece from your loom.

21. Seal the unfinished side by pulling the underside of the rubber band through itself. This will form a knot.

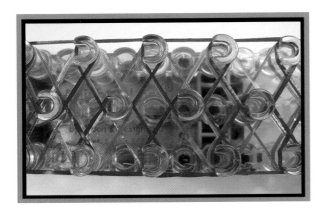

22. Repeat steps 1-9 on your loom, using the same color scheme, to make another bracelet-length piece.

23. Instead of placing a cap band on the last middle peg, this time stretch your cap band from the previous piece over it. When looped, this will connect the two pieces together.

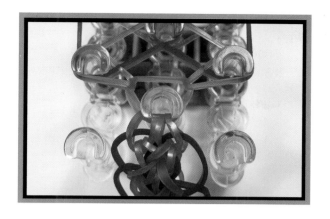

24. Repeat steps 11-21 to loop and finish the second half.

25. Add a pendant to the center for flair.

26. Connect the two ends with a c-clip and you have a fashionable choker!

Rockin' Rainbows
PRO TIPS

Make charms out of designs!
Simply set one repetition of your
Flowers pattern or Starburst
pattern with cap bands...

Loop them as you normally would,
then tie a knot at the top to secure...

Now you have charms to hang off of anything! Make earrings, rings, and dangles for your backpack or purse - the options are endless.

Try making chokers with any design. Use two looms or connect segments and extensions to make something unique.

How To:
HACK YOUR LOOM

At the opposite end of your hook is a pry bar to remove the blue bases from the pegs. Use it to pop them off with ease.

If you are simply doubling the loom for a wrap around bracelet or choker, lay the looms end to end, so the pegs are still offset from one another.

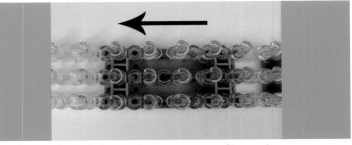

Otherwise, folow the pattern directions exactly. Some designs require parallel pegs in rows, and some require no base at all. Remember to always point your pegs in the same direction, no matter what configuration the design calls for.

Double-Braid

Level: LOOM-a-tic

The "Double-Braid" is a simple design, but requires the use of two looms, modified. You will need to set two rubber bands at a time and it can get tight and tricky!

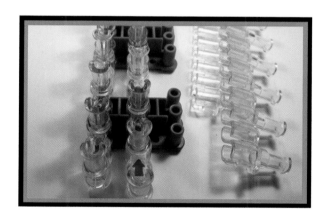

1. Take two looms and join them together, as pictured.

TIP: Make sure all arrows on both looms are pointing in the SAME direction. One side of the peg is for setting and the other is for looping. If it gets mixed up, you will have a difficult time making this bracelet.

2. Pull off the right columns of pegs for simplicity and ease.

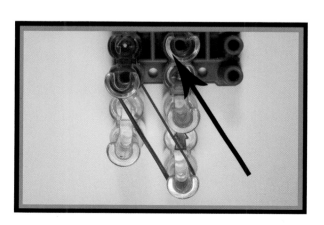

3. Position your loom so the red arrow is pointing away from you. Set your first two rubber bands (of the same color) from the first right (formerly the middle) peg in a long diagonal to the second left peg.

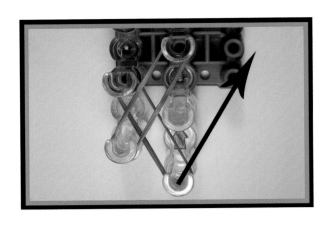

4. Set your second two rubber bands from the first left peg in a long diagonal to the third right peg.

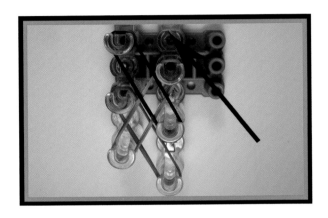

5. Set your third set of rubber bands from the second right peg in a long diagonal to the third left peg.

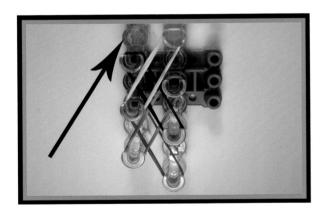

6. Set your fourth set of rubber bands from the second right peg to the fourth right peg.

7. Continue crisscrossing the bands in this manner, all the way up the loom.

8. Check and make sure each peg has two sets of bands on it as you go, so there are no accidental skipped pegs.

9. The first bands to reach the end peg are the final set.

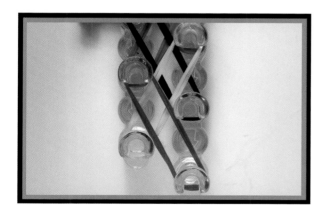

10. Turn your looms around so the red arrows are pointing toward you.

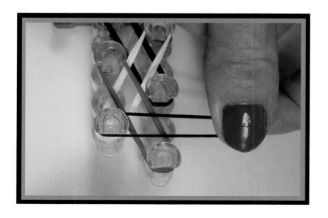

11. Stretch a rubber band from the first left peg, across the middle of the first rubber band.

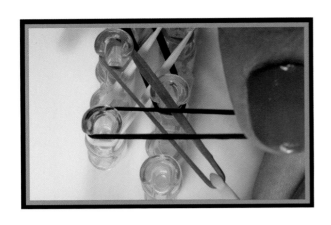

12. Hook the first rubber band while holding on to the one you have stretched out.

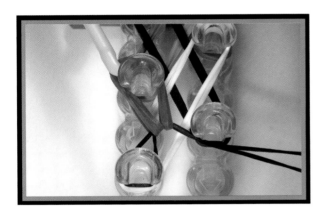

13. Loop it back over the stretched band and back onto the peg it came from.

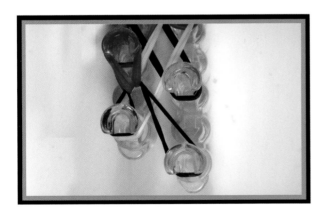

14. Set the stretched band onto the first peg to hold it.

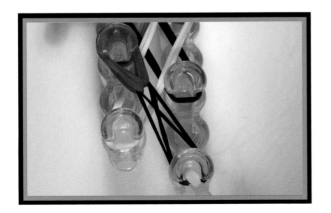

15. Loop the other side of your stretched band over to the first peg to hold the rest of the braid in place.

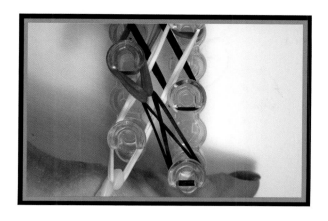

16. Hook the first set of bands (remember there are two, so hook them both) and release from the first left peg.

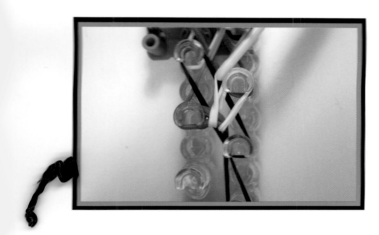

17. Loop them back over to the third right peg, to where the bands came from.

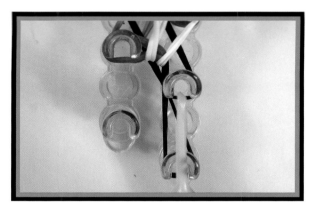

18. Hook the next set of bands on the second right peg.

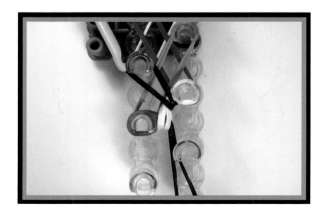

19. Loop them up to the peg they came from.

20. Hook the next set of bands on your left.

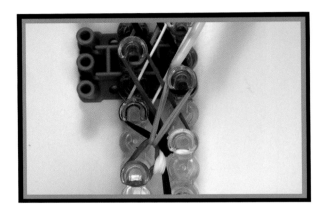

21. Loop them back up to the peg they came from.

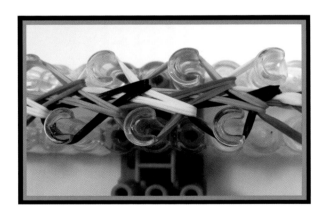

22. Keep braiding each set of bands over each other, all the way down your looms. Left to right and right to left.

23. If done correctly, there will only be one set of folded bands on each peg. If you see other layers below, you missed a loop.

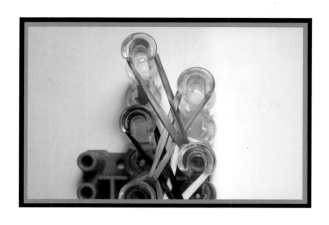

24. End with the final band looped over on itself on the last left peg.

25. Hook all the bands from the last left peg.

26. Loop them around the last right peg.

27. Hook all the bands from the second-to-last left peg.

28. Loop them to the same last right peg.

29. Hook another rubber band through the bands on the last right peg to secure them.

30. Slide the securing band up your hook and pull the bracelet off of the loom. It will be very tight and a little harder than usual to pull off. Stop just before you get to the last single band.

31. Pull the underside of the single band through the overside to create a securing knot.

32. Make the same type of knot with the band on your hook.

33. Secure both ends with a c-clip.

34. Now you have a double-cool "Double-Braid"!

Level: LOOM-a-tic

The "T-Strap" necklace will require the use of two looms and two hooks. It incorporates a "Fishtail" strap into two seperate "Baubles" patterns and uses a charm or pendant.

1. To begin, we will make the center fishtail piece, using two adjacent pegs on one side of your loom. If you have a pendant or charm, pull one rubber band halfway through.

2. Put one side on the peg and twist the rubber band to make a figure eight before wrapping it around the next peg. The first rubber band has to be twisted in this manner or the fishtail will fall apart.

3. Push the figure eight with your charm down on the pegs and place another rubber band (not twisted) over the first.

4. Place a third rubber band over the second, again untwisted. Keep each layer separate on the pegs.

5. Hook the very bottom band on one side.

6. Loop it in front of the peg.

7. Hook the very bottom band on the other side.

8. Loop it in front of the peg.

9. Add another band to the top.

10. Hook the very bottom band on one side.

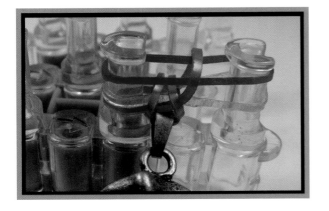

11. Loop it in front of the peg.

12. Hook the very bottom band on the other side.

13. Loop it in front of the peg.

14. Continue adding a top band, and looping each side of the bottom band, and a fishtail braid will begin to emerge.

15. Once you've reached your desired length, use your hook to remove it from the loom and hold each unfinished end secure. Set it aside.

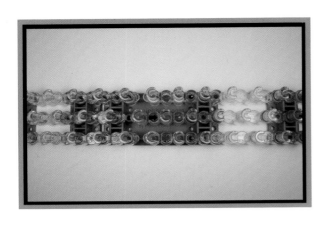

16. To make the baubles portion of the necklace, attach two looms together. Make sure all arrows are pointing the same way and secure.

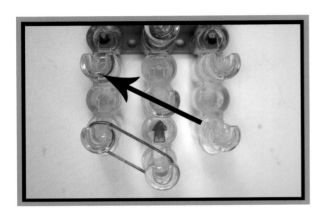

17. Begin with the red arrow pointing away from you. Set your first band from the first middle peg to the first left peg.

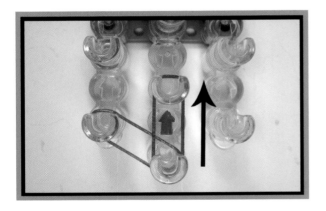

18. Set your second band from the first middle peg to the second middle peg.

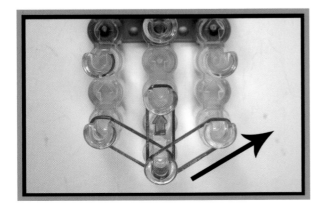

19. Set your third band from the first middle peg to the first right peg.

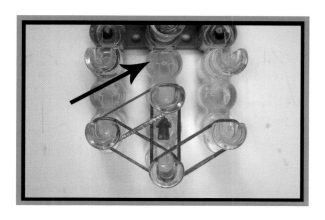

20. Set your fourth band from the first right peg to the second middle peg.

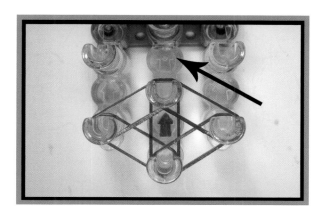

21. Set your fifth band from the first left peg to the second middle peg to complete the bauble.

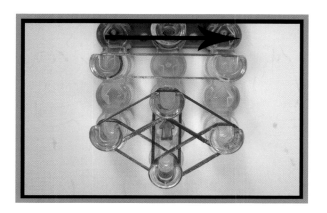

22. A sixth band is placed horizontally from the second left peg to the second right peg.

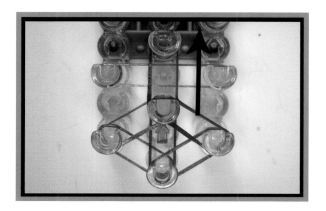

23. Finally, your seventh band, the separator, is placed overlapping the top of your bauble on the second middle peg, to the third middle peg.

24. Begin placing your second bauble from the third middle peg, and repeat the pattern in the exact order all the way to the end of both looms.

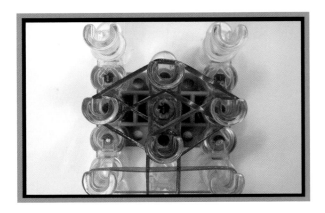

25. Your last bauble should end like this.

26. Place a cap band on the top of your final bauble.

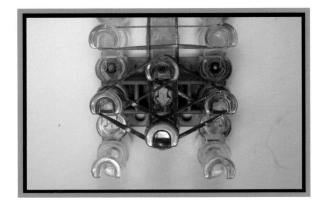

27. Turn your looms around so the arrows are pointing towards you to begin looping.

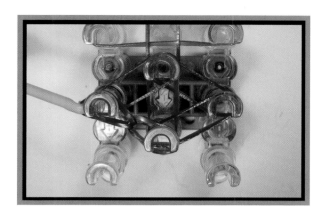

28. Loop the first band from the first center peg to the left.

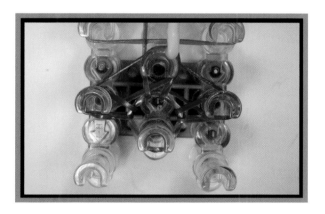

29. Loop the second band from the first center peg to the right.

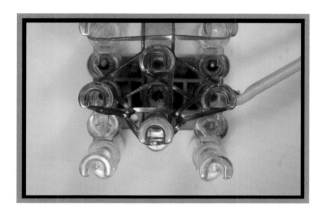

30. Loop the third band up from the first middle peg to the second middle peg.

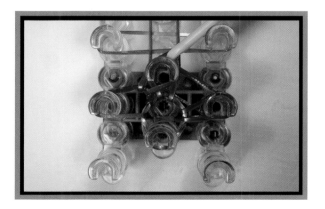

31. Loop the fourth band from the second left peg to the second middle peg.

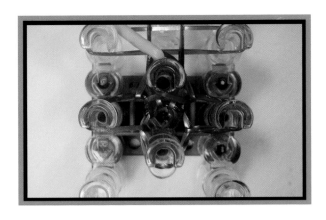

32. Set your fourth band from the second right peg to the second middle peg.

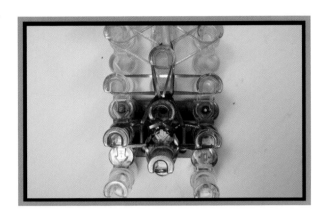

33. Guide your hook into the second middle peg and pull out the bottom band. This will be tricky because there are so many layers wound tightly onto the peg. Loop it up over the next middle peg.

34. Hook your horizontal band from the left side and loop it up to the third middle peg.

35. Hook your horizontal band from the right side and loop it up to the third middle peg.

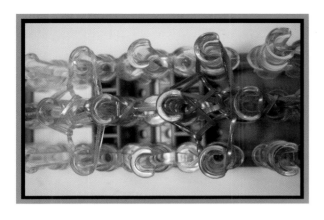

36. Continue looping the pattern in the exact order, all the way down your looms.

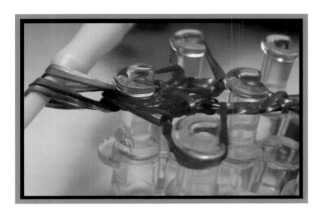

37. Guide two rubber bands through the center of the last peg to secure onto your hook.

38. Pull the necklace off of the loom. Be careful, as the center bands are very tight and can stick to the pegs.

39. Secure the bands on your hook by pulling one side through the other to create a knot. This is one half of your main necklace. Set it aside for a moment to start the other half.

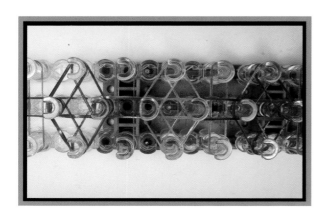

40. Following steps 17-25, lay out another baubles pattern along both looms. Do not add a cap band.

41. Grab your fishtail and pull the finishing knot from the first baubles piece through the unfinished loops. Basically, you want to hang the fishtail off of the double band.

42. Instead of placing a cap band, wrap the finishing loop from your first baubles piece around the final peg to act as the cap band.

43. Begin the same looping process, as in steps 28-35.

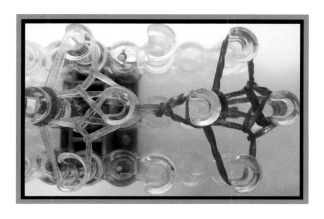

44. Continue looping the exact pattern, all the way down your looms.

45. Again, secure your last ends with two bands.

46. Pull the necklace from your loom. Remember to be careful releasing the middle pegs. They are very tight.

47. Secure the end on your hook by pulling one end of the double band through the other.

48. Place a c-clip to secure both ends of the necklace.

49. Show off your unique "T-Strap" necklace!

6-Point Fishtail

Level: LOOM-a-tic

The "6-Point Fishtail", a.k.a. the "Hexafish," takes the simple fishtail from the last design and adds more dimension. It requires a loom modification and plenty of time.

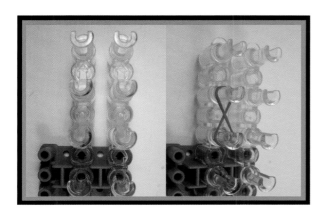

1. Take one side of pegs off of your loom and attach the remaining two so they are parallel. Each column should have three pegs off of the base, for a total of six, as shown. Set your first figure eight across two pegs.

For the first six rubber bands, use a different color than the design. We will be snipping these off at the end and a contrasting color will make it easier to pull apart.

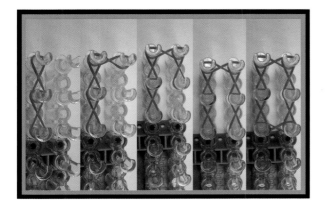

2. Continue setting figure eights around the pegs in a clockwise fashion, overlapping each one as you go. These bands provide a seal at the end, the same way as the simple fishtail.

3. Place your first rubber band (using your chosen colors this time) across all six pegs in a rectangle shape.

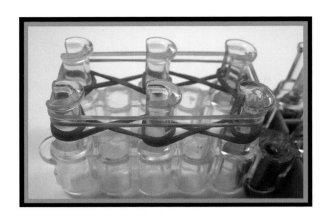

4. Set another rubber band on top. Make sure each is on it's own, separate layer and the bands do not twist or cross.

5. Begin by pulling the bottom two bands from your starting peg. These will be your figure eights from the bottom.

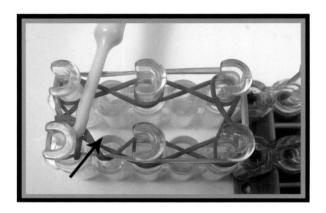

6. Loop them over the peg.

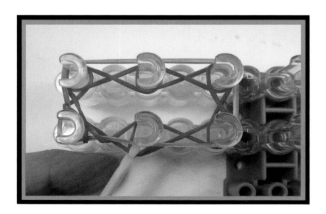

7. Grab the bottom two bands on the next peg.

8. Loop them to the inside of the peg.

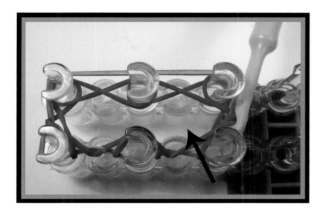

9. Hook the next set of bottom bands.

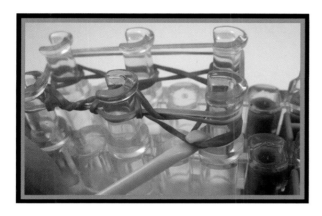

10. Loop them over the peg.

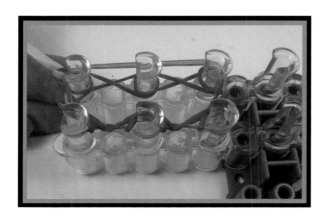

11. Start down the next row and hook the two bottom bands.

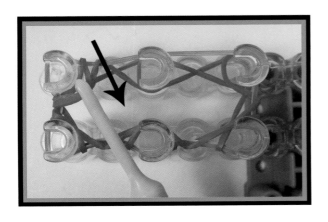

12. Loop them to the inside of the peg.

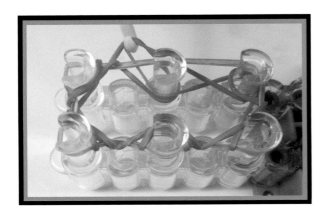

13. Hook the next set of bands.

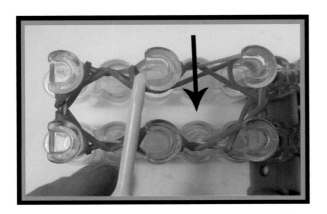

14. Loop them to the inside of the peg.

15. Hook the final two bands that remain on the outside of the peg.

16. Loop them over to the inside of the peg. This completes the seal so your bracelet cannot unravel.

17. Add a fresh rubber band to the top, across all six pegs.

18. Start on any peg, but this time going in a clockwise direction is crucial to the look of your pattern. Hook the very bottom band.

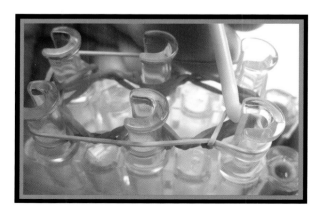

19. Loop it up and over the peg.

20. Hook the next band clockwise from that one and loop it over the peg.

21. Hook the next band clockwise from the previous one and loop it over the peg.

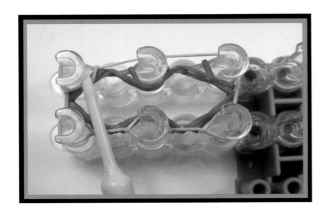

22. Hook the next band clockwise from the previous one and loop it over the peg.

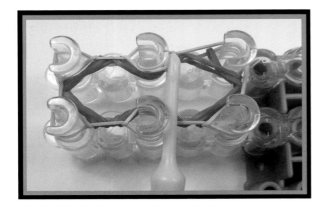

23. Hook the next band clockwise from the previous one and loop it over the peg.

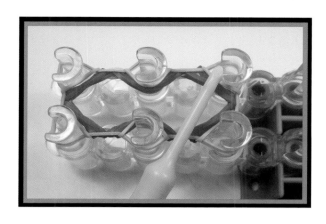

24. End with the final band looped over on itself on the last left peg.

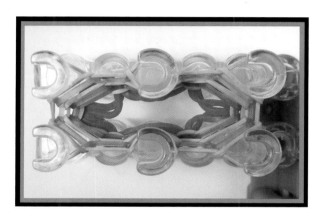

25. Repeat the process of adding a new band and looping the very bottom band over each peg in a clockwise direction. It's just like your basic fishtail with more points. After a few rows, you will see the pattern begin to emerge.

26. Your bracelet will begin to grow down the center of your six pegs and out the bottom.

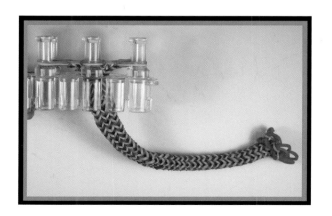

27. Eventually it will be bracelet length and we will need to close up the top. Without adding a new band, loop your lowest band over the pegs so there is only one band left on each.

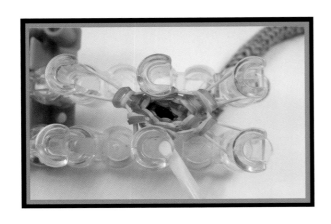

28. Hook the rubber band on one corner peg and loop it to the adjacent middle peg.

29. Hook the band from the outer corner peg and loop it to the adjacent peg.

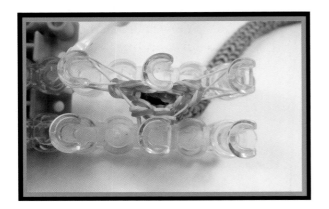

30. Hook the band from your middle peg and loop it to the last corner peg, so now you have a triangle of loops.

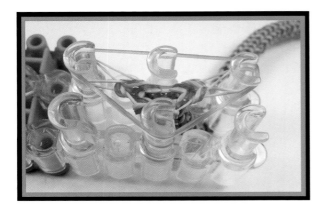

31. Set a new band over the loops, in a triangle shape.

32. Loop the lower bands up and over the first triangle peg.

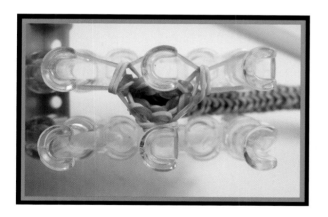

33. Loop the two lowest bands over the next triangle peg.

34. Loop the last lowest bands over the third and final triangle peg. Your triangle band should be the only one holding your bracelet onto the pegs.

35. Loop all of your remaining bands onto one peg.

36. Add your c-clip.

37. Now, the other side has to be closed off the same way. Fish the other side of your bracelet back up through your six pegs.

38. Hook two bands on the outside of your ends. This is where picking a contrasting color comes in handy. There are six sets of these outer bands. Pick any set to start with.

39. Re-attach each set of bands to the loom, peg by peg. The final pegs will be very tight.

40. When finished, your first figure eights will be in the center and all the sets of two original bands will be hooked onto your six pegs, as they would be if you were still weaving.

41. Cut the figure eight bands off.

TIP: If your bracelet isn't long enough, you can add more layers here.

Go back and follow steps 27-34 to close this side the same way you closed the first.

42. Attach the final 3 bands to the other side of your c-clip and marvel at your "6-Point Fishtail"!

Level: LOOM-a-tic

The "Mustache" cuff requires one column of pegs, lots of rubber bands, and time. Instead of a tube-shaped weave, it comes out as a wide weave.

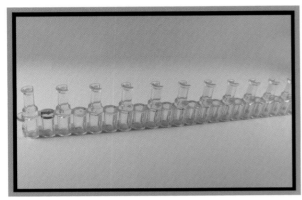

1. Begin by pulling one column of pegs from your loom.

2. With the arrow pointing away from you, lay a row of figure eights on adjacent pegs. Start on the first peg and do not overlap. The last peg will remain empty.

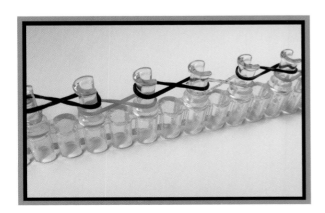

3. Starting from the second peg, lay another row of figure eights on adjacent pegs and do not overlap.

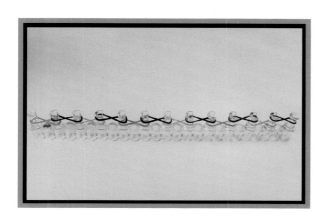

4. Your loom should look like this when done, with two overlapping layers of figure eights. The first peg has one band, the last peg has one band, and the middle pegs have two.

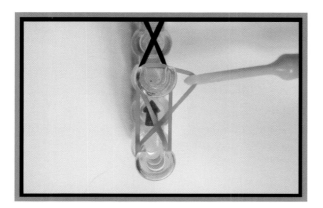

5. Place a new set of bands over the first layer without twisting them.

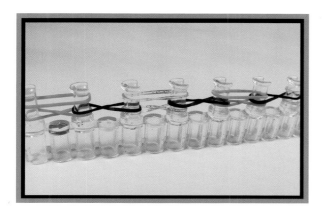

6. Starting at the second peg, hook the bottom band.

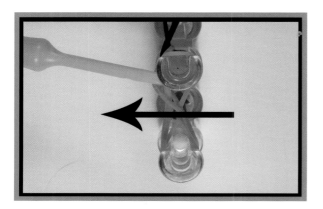

7. Loop it to the other side of the peg.

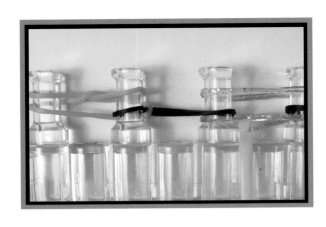

8. Move up to the third peg and hook the lowest band.

9. Loop it to the other side of the peg.

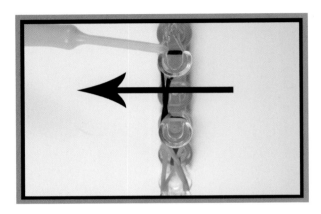

10. Hook the lowest band on the fourth peg.

11. Loop it over to the other side.

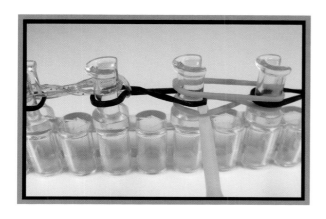

12. Hook the lowest band on the fifth peg.

13. Loop it to the other side.

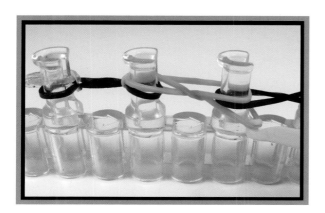

14. Hook the lowest band on the sixth peg.

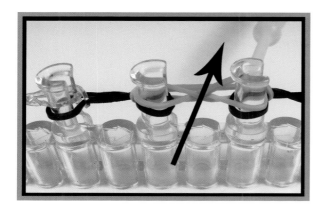

15. Loop it to the other side. Continue hooking and looping the lowest band on each peg, all the way up the loom, to peg 12. Do not loop the last peg.

16. Lay a new column of bands, starting with the second peg, directly over the second row of figure eights. Do not twist.

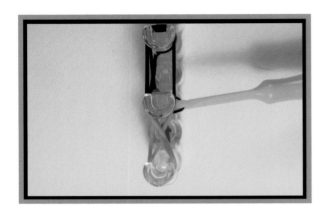

17. Starting at the second peg, hook the lowest band.

18. Loop it to the other side.

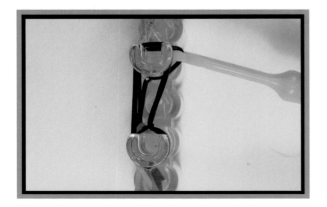

19. Hook the bottom band on the third peg.

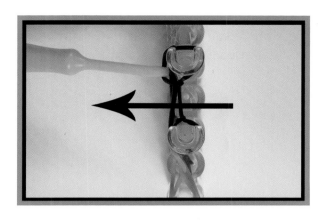

20. Loop it to the other side.

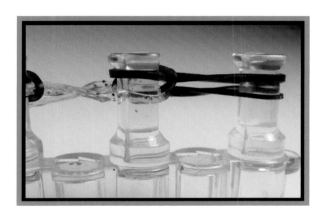

21. Continue hooking and looping the bottom band on each peg, all the way up the loom. Do not loop the last peg.

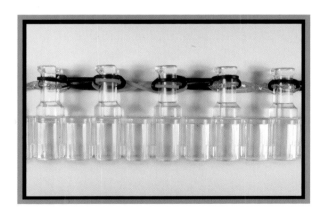

22. Each peg should end up with only two bands apiece after each loop up the loom.

23. Push your bands down in between layers with your hook or fingers. The bands should be low on the pegs so that they don't accidentally fling off mid-loop.

24. Starting with the first peg, lay a new set of bands up your loom. This time, there will be three bands on your first peg, so hook the bottom band on your first peg.

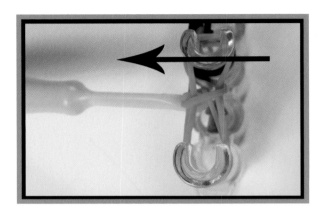

25. Loop it to the other side. It will be loose. This is okay. It will tighten up as the weave grows. On the next pass, when you see three bands on your last peg, you loop that one too. The magic formula is three bands on the peg must always become two.

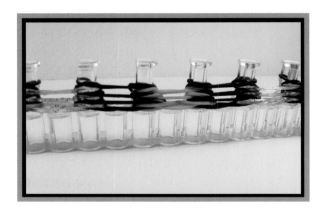

26. Repeat the pattern by adding fresh bands to one layer, looping each peg, then starting over with the next layer. Soon, the pattern will begin to emerge on the other side of your loom.

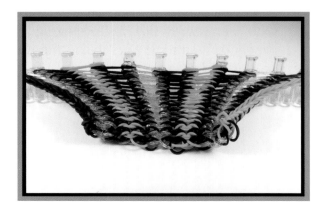

27. Eventually, you will be able to see the mustache pattern. Be patient. Keep layering and looping opposite layers.

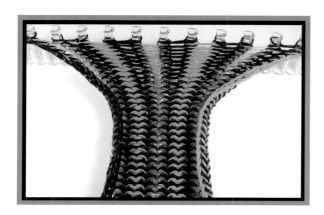

28. Once your weave is cuff length, it is time to finish.

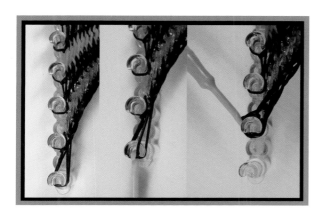

29. Turn your loom around, so the red arrow is pointing toward you. Hook both bands from your first peg and loop them to the second peg.

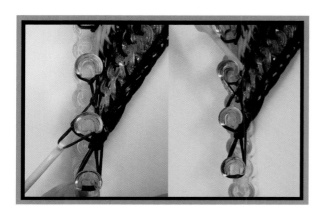

30. Guide your hook into the center of the peg and hook the bottom two bands. Loop them up to the next peg, as if you were completing a "single" bracelet or extending a thick bracelet.

31. Continue hooking the bottom two bands from the center of each peg and looping up, all the way to the last peg. This will prevent the unfinished side of your cuff from unraveling.

32. Fish a rubber band through the loops on the last peg.

33. Add a c-clip to the bands on your hook as well as the very first loop, still on your pegs.

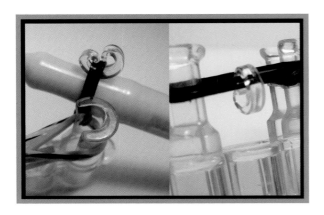

34. Once both c-clips are set, it is safe to remove your cuff from the loom.

35. Fold it in half and attach both c-clips to double bands on the opposite side.

36. Line up your colors and add 2-3 more c-clips for stability.

TIP: Always hook two bands on each side.

37. Now rock your mustache rightside up...

38. ...or inside-out!

LOOM-a-tic Level
PRO TIPS

Add embellishments that rock!

A 6-Point Fishtail makes for a great hook cozy. Simply poke the hook through and wrap the unfinished loops over the top.

Speaking of cute cozies, any cuff design makes a great wrap for your drink bottle!

Try adding new embellishments to the T-Strap. Or add a hook or clasp to make a lanyard.

Explore, Learn, Create, Improvise... Be

Rev-o-LOOM-tionary!